D0384946

HOMELESSNESS

Can We Solve the Problem?

Laurie Rozakis

Twenty-First Century Books

A Division of Henry Holt and Company
New York

Twenty-First Century Books
A division of Henry Holt and Company, Inc.
115 West 18th Street
New York, New York 10011

Henry Holt® and colophon are registered trademarks of Henry Holt and Company, Inc.
Publishers since 1866

Published in Canada by Fitzhenry & Whiteside Ltd.
195 Allstate Parkway, Markham, Ontario L3R 4T8

Printed in the United States of America

Created and produced in association with Blackbirch Graphics, Inc.

Library of Congress Cataloging-in-Publication Data

Rozakis, Laurie.
  Homelessness: can we solve the problem? / Laurie Rozakis. — 1st ed.
      p.   cm. — (Issues of our time)
  Includes bibliographical references and index.
  ISBN 0-8050-3878-7
  1. Homelessness—United States—Juvenile literature. 2. Homelessness—United States—Prevention—Juvenile literature. I. Title. II. Series.
HV4505.R72   1995
362.5'0973—dc20   94-42821
                                                                              CIP

Contents

$\blacksquare$ $\blacksquare$ $\blacksquare$ $\blacksquare$ $\blacksquare$

1

......

The Face of Homelessness

In 1991, Betty Vargas moved from Illinois to New York City with her four young children, believing that the children's father had everything set up for them in New York. But when Vargas arrived, she found no friends, no money—and no home.

She moved in with some relatives and enrolled her children in school. Vargas soon found a temporary job, but the pay wasn't enough to cover both housing and after-school child care. After four months, Vargas's relatives asked her to leave. The family was now homeless. Vargas moved with her children into a shelter—a place that provides emergency housing. They stayed for a year.

Homeless people are people who have no place to live. Here, a homeless man sleeps on a park bench. Homelessness exists in every region of the country and affects Americans of all ages, races, and backgrounds.

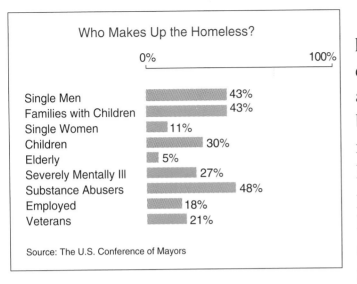

Who Makes Up the Homeless?

Single Men	43%
Families with Children	43%
Single Women	11%
Children	30%
Elderly	5%
Severely Mentally Ill	27%
Substance Abusers	48%
Employed	18%
Veterans	21%

Source: The U.S. Conference of Mayors

Homeless people do not have a permanent residence. Homelessness affects people of all ages, backgrounds, races, and religions. Many of the homeless are hard-working people who lost their jobs. Many Americans are only a few paychecks away from becoming homeless, while others have been poor for a long time. Others have mental illnesses that make it difficult for them to hold on to a job.

No other major industrial nation has such widespread homelessness as the United States. How extensive is the problem? How many people in America are actually without homes?

Answering these basic questions is challenging. Since homeless people have no permanent residence, it is difficult to locate them. They move often, so they cannot be traced easily and many stay in places where the government does not look—in abandoned cars and buildings, under bridges, and in parks.

Before 1987, advocates for the homeless—people working on behalf of this population—believed that more than two million Americans had no place to live. That year, the Urban Institute conducted a survey of homeless people: It found between 355,000 and 445,000 in the United States. Two years later, a writer named Peter H. Rossi conducted his own research. In his book, *Down and Out in America*, Rossi stated that "at least 300,000 people are homeless each night in this country, and possibly as many as 400,000 to 500,000."

For the official 1990 U.S. Census, the government tried to take an accurate count of the number of homeless people in the United States. The census workers focused their count on one night: March 20, 1990. They found 228,621 homeless people in shelters and 49,793 people on the streets. It is likely that some homeless people, sleeping in cars or hiding in alleys, were overlooked.

Whether the number of homeless people is 300,000 or 3 million (as some estimates claim), there are too many people in America who struggle daily to find shelter. Homelessness is one of the most serious problems facing America today.

A U.S. Census taker works through the night to help determine how many people are homeless in America.

Stereotypes About the Homeless

What does a homeless person look like? We all have stereotypes—ideas about people that are not based on facts. How many of the following stereotypes have you heard?

- Some people like the homeless lifestyle.
- Middle-class people can't become homeless.
- Children can't be homeless.
- The homeless are mainly men.
- Homeless people only live in cities.
- Homeless people won't work.
- The homeless are all either mentally ill, alcoholics, or drug abusers.
- The homeless are dangerous.

The Reality of Homelessness

In contrast to the above stereotypes, homeless people include the elderly, young adults, middle-aged people, and children. They are of all races and backgrounds. Some have college degrees; others are high-school dropouts. Some have drug and alcohol problems; others do not. They may be well dressed or ragged, healthy or sick.

What do they all have in common? They are all people who have nowhere to live. Here are some important facts about homelessness:

- Fewer than 6 percent of homeless people chose their lifestyle.

- Most of the homeless are victims of circumstances beyond their control. Many, for example, have lost their jobs because of economic downturns. Some are victims of family violence and are thrown out or must leave their home for their own safety.

- The homeless include men, women, and children. They live in all parts of the United States.

- Many homeless have jobs, but they cannot earn enough to support themselves or their families.

- Figures vary, but about 25 percent of the homeless are mentally ill. Some homeless are substance abusers who also suffer from mental illness.

- The homeless are among the least threatening people in America. They tend to be the victims of crime, not criminals themselves.

People often think that homelessness is a problem only in America's major urban areas. But the homeless seek shelter all over the country—in rural areas, parks, and on beaches.

You can see that stereotypes about homeless people are often wrong. But did you know that these stereotypes can also be dangerous? They cause harm by preventing people from understanding the true causes of homelessness. When we begin to understand the causes of a problem, we can begin to work on possible cures.

Homelessness Is Everywhere

Homelessness exists all across America—not just in big urban centers. Some homeless people sleep in cars parked in city, country, and state parks. In towns and cities, they sleep on park benches, huddle in doorways, and search out public libraries to pass the time in cold weather. In colder months, entire families fill available shelters to overflowing.

Gerald Winterlin's plunge into homelessness began in May 1982, when he was laid off from his job. He was unable to find another job, and soon he also lost his home. Winterlin slept in his car; when the car broke down, he spent his nights in abandoned houses.

Winterlin entered a program for laid-off workers. With the help of a federal Pell Grant—which provides academic aid for low-income people—he enrolled in a two-year college. He did so well that he earned a scholarship to the University of Iowa.

Winterlin was forty-four years old when he gradu-
ated with a nearly perfect A average. Today, he
works as an accountant.

The Elderly
Homeless
Homelessness does not discriminate
on the basis of age. Due to federal programs such
as Social Security and Medicare, most elderly
people in America have some kind of permanent
shelter. Nonetheless, about 5 percent of the homeless are elderly people.

The Goodard-Riverside Project Reach-Out, a
program located in New York City, reported the
case of one elderly couple. The man had been in-
jured in World War II and was not able to earn much
money. In the 1970s, he and his wife moved to
New York City and lived in a series of single-room-
occupancy (SRO) hotels (inexpensive hotels with
rooms meant for one person). Due to advancing age
and the many moves, the woman became confused.
One day, she went out by herself and could not find
her way back. She wandered around the city for
days, finally ending up in Central Park.

Her husband found her there a month later. By
that time, he had run out of money and been thrown
out of the hotel. He moved with his wife to Central
Park. Months later, Project Reach-Out placed them
in a welfare hotel and helped them stay together.

The Single Homeless

Single women make up about 10 percent of the homeless people in America. Some have children; some do not. Many of these women are divorced.

Single men make up about 40 percent of the homeless people in America. About one-third of these men—one-fifth of all homeless people—are veterans (people who have served in the military).

Even for single people with no responsibility for children, the physical discomforts and indignities

Single women become homeless for a variety of reasons. Some have nowhere to turn after a divorce; others may be escaping domestic violence.

The Hidden Homeless

You have probably seen homeless people on the streets where you live. But there are more people whom you may not even realize are homeless. Many of these are families with children, living in shelters. Some of the children may go to your school. Andrew Cuomo, the assistant secretary of Housing and Urban Development in 1994, calls these families "the hidden homeless."

A recent national survey showed that the number of homeless families is increasing in twenty-six major U.S. cities. On Long Island, New York, 366 families were living in shelters in November 1992. A year later, the number had increased to 490 families. And these figures do not include homeless families who may be temporarily staying with relatives or friends.

Homeless children often do not tell their classmates that they and their family are living in a shelter. They are afraid that their classmates will tease them or make fun of them. Other times, parents decide not to send their children to school at all. They may not be able to provide enough clothes or supplies for school. Sometimes, parents need their older children to baby-sit the younger ones while they look for a job.

associated with having no place to live can keep them trapped in homelessness. A young homeless man gave this testimony in the Hearings on Federal Response to Homelessness, held in Los Angeles: "Someone told me that I could get assistance at the Ocean Parks Community Center. I went there and they sent away for my birth certificate. But it's going to take 4-6 weeks.... I have slept at the beach or at parks all together for about 2 months. I'm 20 years old and came to LA [Los Angeles] to look for a job. Since I don't have a place to stay, it's hard to keep up my appearance. I've been washing in sinks. When I go apply for jobs, I get turned down because of my appearance."

Homelessness
Affects Children
Children are the fastest-growing group of homeless. As we have learned, statistics on the homeless vary. But according to one government report, at least 100,000 children are homeless every night. That's enough children to fill all the seats in three big football stadiums. Most of these children are younger than five years old.

There are homeless children of all races and economic backgrounds. Some are homeless because their parents are, but others end up on the streets when they leave home. Officials estimate that about 12,000 children have run away from juvenile facilities. There are also the "throwaways," children who are turned out of their homes due to misbehavior or conflict between their parents. The U.S. Department of Justice reported that 127,000 children were locked out of their homes in 1988 for at least one night and almost half of them had no place to stay.

Homeless young people live in alleys, parks, and abandoned tenements. Peter Brick, a counselor for homeless teenagers, knows the dangers that they face. "If they've been on the street for two weeks, they have a 75 percent chance of getting into some type of illegal activity," Brick says. "That's according to most official figures, but a lot of people who work with them will tell you that it is closer to a 90 percent chance."

Intact families, which are made up of two parents and one or more children, make up about one-fifth of the homeless population, according to some estimates. About 10 percent of the homeless are under age sixteen.

A series of economic hardships can leave entire families homeless. Here, a homeless family begs, or panhandles, on a street in New York City.

Single-parent families make up another fifth of the homeless population. These families are usually headed by women. Often, these women can't work because they have no one to take care of their children. Even if they can get jobs, they do not make enough money to pay for child care.

2

......

How Do People Become Homeless?

There are several different reasons why homelessness is such a big problem in America today. Although some of these reasons are more important than others, each has contributed to the tragedy of the homeless. Economic distress, caused by loss of one's job or high housing costs, is the leading cause of homelessness. Other major factors are divorce, substance abuse, mental illness, natural disasters, and the effects of war. We discuss these far-reaching problems in this chapter.

Joblessness Pretend that one evening a father tells his family that he has lost his job at the airplane factory. The company he works

This New Hampshire man displays a sign illustrating one way many people have found to cope with homelessness—working in exchange for food.

for has laid off many of its workers. The father explains that money will be tight and everyone in the family will have to pull together. The mother has a job in the school cafeteria, but she does not earn enough money to pay all the family's expenses.

The father tries hard to find a new job in the area, but hundreds of people are looking for the same work. He next looks for a job in another state, but people are out of work all over America. Finally, he decides to change careers and begins searching for a job that he can do without a lot of retraining. New jobs are being created every day, but most of them are low-paying jobs in such businesses as retail stores, restaurants, and cleaning. After months of searching, the father cannot find a job that pays enough for the family to meet its bills.

The father qualifies for unemployment insurance, money that some unemployed workers receive from the government. But these payments are still not enough to meet all of the family's bills, even with the mother's income. The family applies for food stamps, coupons that can be used to buy groceries. But this help is still not enough to support the family. In less than a year, the father's unemployment insurance payments end. With little income, the family cannot make its mortgage payments, so the bank takes back (forecloses on) their home. The family is now homeless.

Other

Economic Factors For many Americans, this sort of situation is a reality. More than eight million people are unemployed and without benefits and homelessness is only a few months away. Working people who lose their jobs and their homes are called the "new poor." Many of these people had jobs in manufacturing industries like steel, textiles, and defense. But due to economic difficulties many companies have closed. America has lost two million of these jobs every year since the late 1970s. Many American companies have relocated to countries where it is cheaper to do business.

In 1992, a crowd of 3,000 people showed up to fill out job applications at a new hotel in Chicago. This indicates how high the levels of unemployment are in this country.

In the 1960s, the typical worker could expect his or her income to grow by 50 percent in 10 years. Today, workers can expect their buying power to drop. Even if their incomes rise, the value of their money is less due to inflation, a sharp rise in prices.

According to a recent report by the Children's Defense Fund, the income for families headed by men or women under the age of thirty has declined by 25 percent in the past 15 years. Among Latino people, the decline is 35 percent; among African-Americans, a staggering 50 percent.

The rising cost of health care is another factor that contributes to homelessness. Some families have medical insurance, which covers most of the costs of many medical services. Other families do not have insurance, or it does not cover enough of their medical costs. When a family member without insurance becomes seriously ill, people can lose their homes because of their huge medical bills.

Rising
Housing Costs
We are in the midst of the worst housing crisis Americans have known since the Great Depression of the 1930s. The problem? The difference between what Americans can afford to pay for housing and what it costs to have a home.

After World War II, the government provided help for many families trying to buy a home. Crowds of

returning soldiers seized the chance to get a slice of the "American dream" of home ownership at an affordable price. Between 1945 and 1980, the rate of home ownership went up more than 20 percent. But since then, the number of people able to buy a home has steadily gone down. Young married couples have had the most trouble getting housing. For people between the ages of twenty-five and thirty-four, the rate of home ownership dropped between 1980 and 1989.

The cost of a home has skyrocketed. In the early 1980s, it took about 30 percent of a family's salary to pay the upkeep on a home. Today, it takes more

The rising cost of housing has also contributed to the problem of homelessness. This couple lived in their car in New York's Catskills Mountains for two months after being unable to find affordable housing.

Homeless Population of 10 U.S. Cities	
Rank/City	Total
1. New York	33,830
2. Los Angeles	7,706
3. Chicago	6,764
4. San Francisco	5,569
5. San Diego	4,947
6. Washington, D.C.	4,813
7. Philadelphia	4,485
8. Newark	2,816
9. Seattle	2,539
10. Atlanta	2,491

than 50 percent of a family's annual income to afford shelter. This astonishing rise in prices is due to increasing costs for land, fuel, and wood. The average price of a piece of land has increased 813 percent in the past 20 years, from $5,200 in 1969 to $42,300 in 1989.

What about renting an apartment? A recent study done by Harvard University shows that rents are at an all-time high. Expensive rents make it almost impossible for a family to save the money they need for a down payment on a house. It also makes getting housing even more difficult for the poor. Since fewer middle-class people can afford houses, they now rent apartments. As a result, there are fewer apartments available for the poor.

Along with increases in the cost of housing has come a drop in the type of housing available. For example, due to urban redevelopment the number of single-room-occupancy hotel units has declined dramatically. Many have been converted into condominiums, or knocked down to build stores and other commercial buildings. These SROs are designed for single people on their own. Many times, however, very poor families pack into these small rooms, because they are the last places that they can afford to rent.

Today, few of these rooms remain. In New York City, for example, the number of SROs dropped from 127,000 to 14,000 between 1970 and 1983. In Nashville, the drop was even worse—from 1,680 to just 15! These declines have left many poor people with nowhere to live.

Divorce   During the 1970s, the divorce rate in America was about 3 percent of the total population. By the middle of the 1980s, the percentage of all marriages ending in divorce had doubled. Today, that figure has reached almost 9 percent. As families dissolve and re-form, more housing is needed.

It is very hard to stretch one income to support two households. Most women have custody of their children after a divorce, but maintenance and child-support payments rarely cover all of their expenses. Further, more than 80 percent of divorced women and their children never even get the money that is awarded to them in their divorce settlements. What is the result? More than half of the households headed by women have incomes below the poverty line. Sometimes, these women and their children end up homeless because they cannot afford housing and have no one with whom to live.

Substance Abuse   The 1990 Conference of Mayors found that 38 percent of the homeless have problems with abuse of drugs or alcohol. Drug addictions are expensive. Drug addicts often use up all their money to support their habits. They cannot keep a job and so they end up on the street.

In *Homeless, Health, and Human Needs*, the Institute of Medicine reported that alcoholism is the most frequent single problem among the homeless. The National Institute of Alcohol Abuse and Alcoholism reported that between 20 and 45 percent of the homeless suffer from alcohol-related problems.

Statistics vary, but many show that substance abusers, such as this man, do account for a large percentage of the homeless population.

Some people view alcohol and drug abuse more as a symptom than a cause of homelessness. They argue that homeless people drink and take drugs to escape pain and a situation that they cannot endure.

Mental
Illness   About one-fourth of all homeless people across America suffer from some form of mental illness. One study put the figure at 66 percent. In 1989, scientists at Johns Hopkins University found that 42 percent of homeless men and 49 percent of homeless women studied had serious mental illnesses such as schizophrenia (a psychotic disorder in which people are unable to function socially). An additional 30 percent had less serious mental illnesses. It is now estimated that there are twice as many people with serious mental illness living on the street and in public shelters than there are in psychiatric hospitals.

Why are there so many mentally ill people on the streets? In the 1960s, drugs were created that could help treat some mental illnesses. Some hospitals and health groups decided that people with less serious mental problems, who could be successfully treated, should be allowed to rejoin society. This plan was called deinstitutionalization. The released patients could function in society if they took their drugs and saw their counselors. But the system

How the System Can Fail

According to some estimates, at least fifteen million Americans suffer from a severe mental illness. About one-fifth of these people will have to be treated for their problems at some time during their lives. Even though so many people are affected by mental illness, the mentally ill are still not accepted by society. This is especially true of homeless people who are mentally ill.

We have learned that there are many mentally ill people who have been released from hospitals under the deinstitutionalization plan. For many of these patients, the plan has not worked. Larry Hogue is one of those patients.

Hogue suffers from a mental illness called paranoid/schizophrenia. As part of his illness, he does not trust anyone—not even his own children. During one of his releases from a mental hospital, Hogue was taken in by his adult son. But due to his illness, Hogue found it impossible to establish a relationship. He hears voices in his head. Because of this, Hogue cannot concentrate. The doctors have medications that they can prescribe to quiet the voices, but taking pills tends to remind people that they really are ill and many people suffer side effects.

For years, Larry Hogue has been terrorizing people who live in an uptown neighborhood of Manhattan. Hogue's symptoms are controlled if he takes his medication. But his symptoms become much worse if he takes illegal street drugs, such as crack cocaine. Larry Hogue often forgets to take his medication, but he does take crack. Street drugs don't quiet the voices, but they do cause a burst of energy that can drown out the sound. In fact, some doctors feel that people suffering from paranoid/schizophrenia take street drugs like crack largely to escape the voices they hear in their heads.

Under the influence of crack, Hogue has thrown cinder blocks through church windows and hurled a sixteen-year-old girl in front of a truck. He has been arrested nine times and sent to more than a handful of mental hospitals. In September 1994, a judge released Hogue in less than a week, ruling that he only suffered from an "attitude problem."

People on the Upper West Side are terrified of Hogue. He is big and strong. In order to

did not always work. Most patients did not take their medicine or see their counselors. No one followed up.

A key part of the deinstitutionalization plan was a network of halfway houses—places that provide shelter, medical care, and counseling for many of draw attention to their problem with Hogue, they cite other cases of other homeless mental patients who have "fallen through the cracks" of the system. Such cases include Juan Gonzalez, who killed two people with a sword on New York's Staten Island Ferry and Herbert Mullin, who killed thirteen people near San Francisco. There's also Jim Brady, who shot five people in a shopping mall in Atlanta and Sylvia Seegrist, who shot ten people in a shopping center near Philadelphia. All of these people had serious mental illnesses. All had been told they needed treatment. And none were getting any help at all.

The mental health system is not set up to handle people like Larry Hogue. The crack cocaine wears off in a few hours, often before Hogue is even released from jail. At that point, Hogue appears fine, so he cannot be put in a hospital against his will. Hogue is typical of homeless mental patients. A recent survey found that on any day, there are about 30,700 persons with schizophrenia or manic-depressive illness among the 426,000 people in America's jails. Many of these mentally ill patients are not charged with any crime. They are merely being held in jail because they have nowhere else to go. In most cases, they are waiting for a bed in a state mental hospital. In seventeen states it is legal to hold a mentally ill person in jail without any charges against him or her. In other cases, the police sometimes arrest mentally ill homeless people on a minor charge just to get them off the streets for their own protection and safety. This happens so often that there is even a name for it— "mercy booking."

Doctors reveal another side of the story. "Hogue is always discharged because he's a pain in the neck," said one doctor. "No one is using the available legal authority [to hold him] because no one wants Hogue on his ward." A study in Massachusetts showed that nearly 30 percent of the mentally ill patients released from state mental hospitals become homeless within six months; in Ohio, the figure was nearly 40 percent.

As people like Larry Hogue have discovered, the system doesn't have the resources to follow-up on his care. There just aren't enough doctors, nurses, and hospitals.

The system failed Larry Hogue. And it is failing thousands of homeless mentally ill people like him.

these released patients. However, funding was not available and these halfway houses were never built. The mental patients were left to fend for themselves and many ended up homeless.

How many patients have actually been discharged? Between 1955 and 1986, the number of places in state mental hospitals declined from 552,000 to 108,000. This trend has only gotten worse, as doctors are under more pressure to discharge mental patients to save money.

Natural Disasters

Homelessness also occurs as a result of natural disasters. For example, a family's house can be destroyed by fire. If the adults have jobs and insurance to cover some or most of the loss, the

The 1993 Midwest Flood

The United States had a number of devastating natural disasters in the late 1980s and early 1990s: blizzards, droughts, earthquakes, hurricanes, and several of the hottest summers ever. But as tragic as these disasters were, none could compare to the great flood of 1993 along the Mississippi and Missouri rivers.

For months, rains lashed the upper Midwest. Rivers swelled at unbelievable rates: In Papillion, Nebraska, one river rose a full inch in just six minutes. Levees burst wide open, soaked and pounded for weeks by the rushing waters. The water poured through the openings with a raging roar that sounded like a freight train. Stretches of highway and railroad tracks disappeared, sunk deep in the swirling waters. The rush of water led to frantic evacuations. On July 22, 1993, 150 people were hurried out of their homes in St. Charles County, Missouri, in the middle of the night. They joined the 8,000 already homeless in St. Charles County alone.

When it was over, eight million acres were flooded. Twelve million were too soaked to be seeded. Parts of Illinois, Iowa, Kansas, Minnesota, Missouri, Nebraska, North Dakota, South Dakota, and Wisconsin were declared federal disaster areas. In many places, the floodwater washed dirt into the clean water supply. Farm pesticides and industrial chemicals were also carried by the water. "Think of all this stuff making a witches' brew of new compounds," said Kevin Coyle, president of an environmental group. "There has never been a flood this bad. People just don't know what will happen."

All told, the damage was estimated to cost about $8 billion and thousands were left homeless. With whole towns underwater for weeks, many workers lost their jobs and their homes.

Natural disasters have caused thousands of people to lose their homes. This man suffered the loss of his home in Kendall, Florida, during Hurricane Andrew in 1992.

family can be relocated within a few days or weeks. But if a family lacks these resources, homelessness can occur.

Hurricane Andrew, one of the worst natural disasters in U.S. history, left nearly 300,000 people homeless in August 1992. Thousands of volunteers flocked to South Florida to help repair the estimated $30 billion in damage. So far, volunteers have worked on about 7,000 homes. But thousands of people are still without permanent housing.

Blizzards, floods, and earthquakes can also be devastating. On October 17, minutes before the third game of the 1989 World Series, an earthquake struck the San Francisco Bay area. At least 59 people were killed, and 8,000 left homeless. The floods in the midwestern United States in 1993 left 50 dead and 70,000 homeless.

Effects
of War
Some reports estimate that about 20 percent of all homeless people are men who fought in America's wars. Many people assume that most of these men are Vietnam veterans, but this is not true. Most of the homeless veterans are men who joined the military during the 1970s and 1980s. Many come from poor and damaged families. Often, these men enlisted in order to get away from their troubled backgrounds and learn useful job skills. But many of them did not acquire the useful skills they needed, and when they left the service, they found that they could not get jobs.

Veterans have higher rates of mental illness and substance abuse than other homeless people. A number have posttraumatic stress disorder, a mental illness caused by battle experiences. The symptoms include sensitivity to noise and self-destructive behavior and make it almost impossible for its sufferers to work.

Decline in Federal Programs

The poverty rate is the part of the population whose income falls below the government's official poverty level. In 1991, 35.7 million Americans were living below the poverty level. This means that one out of every seven Americans is officially "poor." The number of poor children is even more frightening. One out of every four children live in poverty.

Many of these people depend on some form of government aid to survive. In 1992, for example, the government paid a total of $43 billion in aid to the poor. That sounds like a lot of money, but it is actually far less than in previous years. In 1981, for instance, the government paid $33 billion on low-income housing alone. But ten years later, that amount had been cut by $25 billion. The government has also slashed the number of new apartments that it builds for the poor. In the 1970s, more than 200,000 apartments were built each year; in 1990, fewer than 15,000 were built. The minimum wage and Aid for Dependent Children benefits are also falling far below the level of inflation.

3

What Problems Do the Homeless Face?

Think about waking up every day in a different place. You don't know where you will get food. You don't know how you will stay safe. You don't know where you will sleep that night. These are among the many problems that the homeless face. In this chapter, we look at these problems more closely.

Staying Healthy Homeless people suffer from a number of serious health problems caused by their lack of a home. Sleeping outdoors in the

The winter months pose a serious threat to homeless people and many cities create emergency shelters. This homeless man, in Washington, D.C., pulls a blanket loaded with his belongings across Lafayette Park.

extreme heat and cold can be deadly. The homeless are at greater risk of being victims of attacks and accidents. They rarely have a chance to wash or change their clothes, which can lead to skin problems such as boils and ulcers. The homeless often must stand or sit for long periods of time, which can cause severe problems with blood circulation. Many are victims of dangerous viral infections, such as tuberculosis. The stress of being homeless may also aggravate high blood pressure and

Because homeless people have difficulty getting medical care, many shelters offer free clinics that provide necessary medical treatment.

diabetes. Finally, the cheap food the homeless often eat is generally high in calories and fat and low in nutrition. This causes many health problems, especially malnutrition, a condition that occurs when people don't get enough good food to eat.

It is difficult for the homeless to get medical care. They often don't have a way to get to a doctor or the money to afford to go. Some homeless people are unwilling to seek medical care. They are afraid they will be hurt or have their possessions stolen. The lack of medical care is especially dangerous for those suffering from conditions such as high blood pressure, diabetes, and tuberculosis.

Staying

Safe Homeless people have a hard time staying safe because many are unable to defend themselves or run away quickly enough. Weakened by not eating enough, illness, and lack of sleep, they are easy prey for attackers. They face dangers on the streets and in shelters. Prejudice against the homeless leads many people to pay little attention to their complaints, both during and after an attack. The homeless are easy to attack because they are defenseless and powerless. Sometimes, aggressive people deliberately attack the homeless. Crimes against homeless street people are common.

Larry Nelson, a twenty-year-old homeless man in Los Angeles, explained the dangers on the street this way: "My possessions [blanket, backpack, and sleeping bag] were all stolen. I was also robbed. That's how I lost my I.D. [identification]. I feel depressed. I feel let down.... I also got my left eye kicked in by an angry man. I was on a bus when this happened.... They had to reconstruct my cheek bone and the bone around my eye."

Shelters can also be very dangerous places to stay because the crowded conditions make it difficult to escape attack. The beds are side by side, perhaps separated only by a sheet. It is easy to rob or attack a sleeping person. In several 1994 surveys, 33 to 66 percent of homeless people living in shelters reported having been the victim of a crime within the previous six months. They were attacked by outsiders, other shelter residents, staff, or police. Betty Vargas has memories of her stay at a shelter.

"Every morning the guard would turn on the floodlights at 6:00 A.M. to welcome another day of misery. I never got much sleep; profanity spurted from the mouths of men, women and children from sunup well into the night. My fear of rodents and cockroaches crawling on my two daughters, ages 5 and 9, and my 7-year-old twin sons kept me awake too. This was our first taste of life in a New York City shelter...."

Are the homeless a threat to society? "Yes," said 49 percent of the people who responded to a 1993 survey by *Glamour* magazine. In 1993, a homeless drug abuser murdered an eighty-year-old woman in New York City. This sparked fears that the homeless are dangerous. Others argue that the homeless drive away tourists and shoppers.

People who work with the homeless, however, argue that homeless people are actually less likely to commit violent crimes than are people with permanent addresses. Officials often find that the most serious crimes that the homeless commit are shoplifting and breaking into buildings to find a place to sleep. Only a small number of the homeless have been arrested for assault and murder.

Finding Shelter

"There are three main causes for homelessness: housing, housing, and housing." So claims Robert Hayes, a person who often helps the

This New York City shelter provides refuge for hundreds of needy people. Shelters offer a solution to housing the homeless, however, many are unsafe and unsanitary.

homeless. Homeless people must find a place to stay every night. They have only a few options: shelters, welfare hotels, public parks, cars, low-income housing, and abandoned buildings.

According to a survey conducted by the U.S. government, about 350,000 homeless people stay in shelters every night. Shelters are either privately funded or are supported by state or federal grants. A recent survey of twenty-nine major cities by the U.S. Conference of Mayors revealed that requests for emergency shelter increased by 14 percent in 1992. Almost one-quarter of those requests could not be met.

A shelter may be simply one huge room, with up to 1,000 cots lined up in rows like soldiers. There is little privacy. Other shelters may be in small basement rooms or old auditoriums. Some shelters are clean, warm, and well run. Others are dirty, noisy, and badly organized. Many homeless people prefer the streets to the shelters. As one homeless man said, "The police took me off the subway and to the Men's Shelter a few months back, but I couldn't stay. I am 68 years old and can't defend myself down there...."

Hotels used to house homeless people are dirty and dangerous. They are often located in very unsafe areas in cities. Here's how a homeless woman in Los Angeles described her stay in a welfare hotel:

"I had my room broken into, my food stamps stolen.... The police told me not to leave my room after dark because it's so dangerous where I live.... I pay $220 a month for rent for a room 10 by 10. And I have to share the toilet and shower with 79

Because of the dangers of living in a shelter, this homeless man would rather live in the park of San Francisco's Civic Center Plaza.

other rooms.... The toilets are always so filthy and the showers so nasty I feel dirtier after I get out than when I got in.... Even when the water is warm, it's only lukewarm, it's never hot.... And when I complain to the manager, she tells me, if I don't like it to get out. So I have a place to stay, but I'm still homeless."

Streets and parks have their own dangers, but many homeless people prefer them to shelters and welfare hotels. In a park, homeless people can pick the safest place to sleep. They can move away quickly when danger comes. In a park, a homeless person can have a personal space and privacy that cannot be found in a shelter. For many homeless, then, the parks offer a freedom not possible in a shelter.

Low-income housing is often in very bad condition. Many of the apartments have had fires but are left unrepaired. They also are often located in very unsafe areas. Why do people live in such dangerous places? Money. An apartment in the projects can cost as little as $60 a month, with heat and electricity included.

Some homeless people choose to move into run-down, abandoned buildings. This practice is called squatting, and it is against the law. Nonetheless, homeless people continue to do it; some even start to repair these buildings.

Finding
Schooling
Any child living in the United States is guaranteed an education. According to the Federal Compulsory Attendance Law, no child can be denied "a free and appropriate education." Children do not have to present any citizenship or residency documents to attend school; in fact, it is illegal to ask a child for proof that he or she is an American citizen or has a home.

In many areas, homeless children have a choice of schools. When they move, they can still attend their former school. This way, even if they move a lot, they do not have to get used to a new school. In New York State, the school district provides transportation to help the child get to school.

When a child is homeless, however, he or she has less chance of doing well in school. A 1986 study found that almost half of homeless preschoolers had at least one serious developmental problem. More than one-third had delayed language development.

Homeless young people also often face prejudice. Thirteen-year-old Melissa Rodriguez, living in the H.E.L.P./Suffolk, New York, shelter, described her education: "When I started school out here, a lot of kids in my school were making fun of me by saying that I'm poor or laughing at me and sometimes they would start screaming out 'H.E.L.P./Suffolk' on the bus or in the halls."

Safe Zones for the Homeless in Miami, Florida

"When I'm out with my three-year-old daughter in the park, I shouldn't have to worry about whether she'll notice what the man by the tree is doing." So wrote a woman in response to a 1993 survey on homelessness conducted by *Glamour* magazine. In fact, a whopping 73 percent of the people surveyed responded that homeless people should not be allowed to bathe and relieve themselves in public.

All over America the homeless have been chased out of parks, shopping malls, and city streets. Most people quietly move on, but the homeless in Miami decided to take action. In 1988, the American Civil Liberties Union (ACLU) filed a lawsuit on behalf of the homeless. The suit charges that Miami police arrested homeless people to make sure that they didn't offend workers, shoppers, and tourists. The ACLU wants the homeless to be given money for the problems that this approach has caused them.

The lawsuit was settled on November 16, 1993. That day, Federal District Court judge C. Clyde Atkins agreed with the ACLU: He said that the City of Miami had indeed violated the rights of 6,000 homeless people. He ordered the City of Miami to create two "safe zones" for homeless people. They had to be places where the homeless could care for themselves safely. The U.S. Constitution guarantees even those people "who are forced to live in public" basic rights, Atkins ruled. These include the right to eat, sleep, cook, and wash. Atkins directed lawyers for the homeless and the City of Miami to work together to find the best places to set up the safe zones. He said that the places should be close to "feeding programs, health clinics and other services."

Most people working to help the homeless applauded the judge's decision. "We have a lot of very poor people in our society today who have no choice but to perform life functions outside in public," said Joan Alker, the assistant director for the National Coalition for the Homeless. "The judge's decision says that you can't punish people for simply being poor."

However, some advocates for the homeless did not agree. They are afraid that the safe zones could hurt the homeless in the long run by taking their problems out of the public eye. If people do not see the problem, they argue, they will assume that it has gone away.

Escaping Homelessness

It is not easy to escape from homelessness. About one-fifth of all homeless people work at a full-time or part-time job. Imagine that you are homeless and manage to get a job. It

Miami's "safe zones" have enabled this young Florida man to stay in his plywood shack under Interstate 395 without the fear of being evicted.

pays minimum wage, $4.25 per hour. If you work full time (40 hours a week), you will earn only $170 per week. The least expensive apartment in a suburban area costs around $300 a month; in a city, the price can be double.

When you rent an apartment, you usually have to give the landlord at least one month's extra rent. This is called a security deposit, because it is meant to protect the landlord against damage to the apartment. But how can you save enough money for the security deposit? Your salary has to be able to pay for food, clothing, child care, transportation, medical care—and rent. Minimum-wage jobs just do not pay enough to help a homeless person afford decent housing.

To get an apartment or a job, you often need to provide a reference. This is a personal recommendation that you are a trustworthy person. The homeless often have a very hard time getting references. This can prevent them from getting good jobs or places to live.

Public opinion is another obstacle for the homeless. Today, many people ignore the homeless. Others fear and resent them. In New York City, police threw the homeless out of Penn Station and tore down their makeshift shelters in Tompkins Square Park. In 1990, voters in Washington, D.C., abolished the right-to-shelter law. Local police immediately began to arrest beggars. A year later, Atlanta's mayor, Maynard Jackson, asked the City Council to arrest anyone found sleeping in empty buildings. Penalties included up to sixty days in jail and fines.

What about places recognized for their compassion for the homeless? Even here there has been a sharp change in attitude. For example, the police in Berkeley, California, used to ignore the homeless people sleeping in People's Park. Now the police are under orders to chase them out. "Instead of attacking the problem of homelessness, some cities are now attacking homeless people themselves," says Maria Foscarinas, director of the National Law Center on Poverty and Homelessness.

In June 1991, police forcibly removed homeless people from Tompkins Square Park in New York City.

4

What Can Be Done?

In 1967, a senior federal government official approached the Smithsonian Institute with an unusual idea. He wanted the famous Washington, D.C., museum to place on exhibit an old crumbling "railroad flat" tenement in the National Museum of American History. These railroad flats were small apartments, each room in a row off a central hallway. Since the government's "War on Poverty" programs were going to eliminate poverty soon, the official reasoned, it would be a good idea to save a reminder of it for future generations.

Unfortunately, there is no need to place such a tenement in a museum. Such run-down apartments are still all around us, in every city in America.

Actions are being taken to improve the homeless situation in America. Here, former president Jimmy Carter, and his wife, Rosalynn, work with Habitat for Humanity to build houses for the homeless.

What Can the Government Do?

November 28, 1993, was a bitterly cold night. The temperature sank into the low thirties, and a bitter wind whipped through the bare trees. Yetta Adams lay down to sleep at a bus shelter in Washington, D.C. To protect herself against the freezing wind, Adams covered herself with a tattered old blanket. Her pillow? It was a crumpled paper bag.

The next morning, Adams was found dead. Her frozen body was lying on a bench across the street from the very government agency that is supposed to help the homeless—the Department of Housing and Urban Development (HUD). Few people noticed Adams's death. President Bill Clinton has

HUD secretary Henry Cisneros has worked hard to develop concrete solutions to help alleviate the serious problem of homelessness in America.

called homelessness "our most embarrassing social problem," but the U.S. government has yet to come up with ways to help the homeless that work.

HUD secretary Henry Cisneros is trying to change that. In February 1994, Cisneros sent Clinton a report calling for greatly increased spending for the homeless. Cisneros wants the money spent to build more houses and apartments for the poor and to expand mental health care and drug treatment programs for the homeless.

Programs to help homeless veterans are currently being evaluated to see how to improve the aid given to veterans.

Many homeless people are veterans. Advocates for the homeless point out that the government already has programs in place to help this part of the homeless population. Expanding these programs could help a great many people for relatively little

One Person Can Make a Difference!

In 1987, Beth Spence, the coordinator of Covenant House's Rural Housing Program, took a trip through the Virginia countryside. She found people living in tin shacks, in old buses and abandoned cars, and in dirt-floor huts. "A large number of the rural poor lived in places that looked like houses but that didn't protect them from the elements. When something happened to these fragile places—a fire, a flood—people often ended up on city streets," said Spence.

Spence began working with people in two small villages. She wanted to set up building projects for families at risk of becoming homeless. How many people were affected? Eighty percent of the people in both villages were just one paycheck away from poverty. Town meetings were called, grants written to receive funds, committees established, residents trained in recordkeeping, and craftspeople found to do the actual building.

The first house went to a family whose home was in such poor shape that it fell apart around them. Then, three months later, the group built a home for a family who had lost theirs to fire and were too poor to get a bank loan to rebuild.

Each house transforms the lives of the towns-people. "This has shown me that many things are possible if we allow low-income people to make decisions in their communities," concluded Spence. "I've learned: You just have to work on problems a little bit at a time; take small steps."

money. For example, the Veterans Administration (VA) could increase its outreach programs to the homeless. It could provide job-counseling services in the larger shelters and hire more people to help veterans suffering from mental illness and substance abuse. In addition, the VA could help homeless veterans with their medical and legal problems.

One of the most hotly debated federal programs concerns replacing welfare with "Workfare." Under this proposal, people would have to hold jobs to get federal assistance. When he was governor, Clinton wanted to set a two-year cap on welfare benefits.

Here's what he said: "I want to erase the shame of welfare for good by restoring a simple, dignified principle: No one who can work can stay on welfare forever." Governor Clinton and Senator Daniel Patrick Moynihan applied pressure and helped push the Family Support Act through Congress in 1988. This bill forced the states to help more people on welfare enter job-training programs and increased federal money for these programs.

Many other politicians have supported the idea of replacing welfare with Workfare. In 1988, Wisconsin Governor Tommy G. Thompson created a "Learnfare" program. Parents on federal assistance would lose money if their children missed too many days of school. Aid is cut $100 a month if a child misses two days of school in a month after ten unexcused absences. In 1991, thirty-nine states either cut welfare benefits or did not increase them to match the higher cost of living. Many people feel that welfare makes poverty and homelessness worse by taking away people's motivation to work. It also encourages families to break up, they claim, and women to have more children.

In 1949, the government passed the Housing Act. It called for "a decent home and a suitable living environment" for all Americans. It did not, however, describe how to achieve these goals. In fact, America is the only industrialized country in the world that does not have a national housing policy. Different leaders are trying to find ways to make the goals of the Housing Act a reality. The National Urban Coalition's Low-Income Housing Task Force, for example, argues that the government can play a crucial role in helping the homeless by restoring HUD's budget to $30 billion and funding a community-based housing program.

Critics have pointed to four places where the government can make a big difference:

• Build more low and middle-income housing. At least five million new homes are needed in the 1990s.

• Support the existing public housing that is at risk of being lost. More than one million apartments and two million private homes are so run down that they could be condemned.

• Give working-class and lower-income people chances to own their own homes by lowering the amount of interest that they would be charged to get mortgages.

• Make sure that banks don't overcharge for mortgages or discriminate against minorities.

What Can the Homeless People Do?
Some homeless people earn some money by working street jobs. These jobs include washing car windshields and sweeping

storefronts. Such jobs sometimes give people just enough money for inexpensive meals, but they rarely provide enough earnings to escape homelessness. As a result, many homeless people turn to the community for support. Homeless people get help from the community in the form of shelters, food pantries, and clothing drives.

In an effort to help themselves, a resourceful group of homeless people in Los Angeles, California, built this dome village with the financial help of the community.

Many of the homeless are forming their own communities. "Justiceville" is a small Los Angeles community of eighteen fiberglass homes. They cost $6,500 each and are shaped like igloos. People who live there are in charge of everything from maintenance to staffing the community kitchen. A group of homeless people built this community themselves. The city gave them the land and a private foundation gave them the money. "We've got to help ourselves before anybody else will," said Justiceville resident Eri Burns.

What Can Citizens Do?

One way to help the homeless is to learn about them and their problems. Share what you know with others; help them to separate facts from stereotypes.

All across the United States, citizens are banding together to run soup kitchens, shelters, and neighborhood associations for the homeless. Some fix up abandoned buildings and build new homes for the poor. They pressure local leaders to protect tenants from being unfairly evicted from their apartments. In addition, they help make sure that health and safety laws are followed, especially where the poor are concerned. To keep neighborhoods vital, they convince businesses to open up offices and stores in low-income neighborhoods. They write newspaper

An organization in Berkeley, California, raises funds that benefit the homeless and distributes vouchers that people can redeem for food and other services.

and magazine articles on the plight of the homeless and pressure banks to lend money to poor people.

More than 200,000 people took part in the October 1989 Housing Now march in Washington, D.C. A group called Partnership for the Homeless runs shelters in churches and synagogues across the country. People from the community cook and serve the meals. In 1991, the Hotel Workers Union set up a contract that requires Boston hotels to contribute $1.20 a day to a fund that the union members

Common Meals has helped to end the cycle of homelessness and joblessness in Seattle. About 80 percent of their graduates are placed in jobs in the food industry.

will use to provide housing assistance to its members. The Bricklayers Union is building nonprofit housing in several cities. In Seattle, the nonprofit group Common Meals trains homeless people to be chefs and waiters and then gets them jobs in local restaurants.

In 1968, a group of students at Northport High School in Long Island, New York, formed a club called Students for 60,000 (the estimated number of homeless people in New York City at the time). The club holds clothing drives and raises funds to lend to homeless families who need money for security deposits. This year, the club is raising money for Habitat for Humanity. This is a national group whose members build houses for low-income families. The community chapters of Habitat act as banks and provide no-interest loans on the houses built. As families make their monthly payments, the money is used to build another house. The average Habitat for Humanity home costs $30,000 to build and involves 500 hours of work.

If you hear about a law or policy regarding the homeless that interests you, write to your local elected officials. To learn more about the homeless or to volunteer your help, write to the following organizations for information:

Child Welfare League of America
440 1st Street, NW, Suite 310
Washington, DC 20001

Coalition for the Homeless
89 Chambers Street, 3rd Floor
New York, NY 10007

Habitat for Humanity
121 Habitat Street
Americus, GA 31709-3498
(800) 334-3308

The National Resource Center on Homelessness and
Mental Illness
262 Delaware Avenue
Delmar, NY 12054
(800) 444-7415

National Student Campaign Against Hunger and
Homelessness
29 Temple Place
Boston, MA 02111
(800) 664-8647

The Partnership for the Homeless
305 7th Avenue, 13th Floor
New York, NY 10001

Glossary

addiction A physical or psychological need for substances like drugs or alcohol.

census An official count of the number of people who live in a specific area.

deinstitutionalization The practice of releasing patients from mental hospitals.

displaced workers People trained for jobs that no longer exist.

evict To force people to leave an apartment because they do not pay the rent.

food stamps Coupons from the federal government that people can use to buy food.

foreclosure When the bank takes back a home because the owners cannot pay back the money that they borrowed to buy it.

halfway houses Shelters for patients released from mental hospitals; they offer counseling, medical services, and shelter.

inflation A sharp rise in prices.

malnutrition A condition that occurs when people don't get enough of the proper foods to eat.

medical insurance Insurance that covers most or all of the cost of medical care.

new poor Working-class people pushed into poverty because they lose their jobs or because their jobs do not pay enough to support them.

posttraumatic stress disorder A mental illness that some war veterans suffer as a result of battle experiences

security deposit Money given to a landlord that remains on deposit until the tenants leave an apartment. The money is returned if the apartment is not damaged.

shelters Emergency housing for homeless people.

single-room-occupancy hotels Inexpensive hotels with rooms designed for single people.

squatter A person who illegally moves into a building.

stereotypes Fixed ideas of how people look and act that are not based on fact.

unemployment insurance Money that some unemployed workers receive from the government.

welfare Government aid for people who are poor or unemployed.

For Further Reading

Beckelman, Laurie. *The Facts About the Homeless.* New York: Crestwood House, 1989.

Davis, Bertha. *Poverty in America: What We Do About It.* New York: Franklin Watts, 1991.

Jones-Seymour, Carole. *Homelessness.* New York: New Discovery Books, 1993.

Kosof, Anna. *Homeless in America.* New York: Franklin Watts, 1988.

Kroloff, Charles. *54 Ways You Can Help the Homeless.* New York: Macmillan, 1993.

Landau, Elaine. *The Homeless.* New York: Simon and Schuster, 1987.

Marx, Doug. *The Homeless.* Vero Beach, FL: Rourke, 1990.

O'Neill, Terry. *The Homeless: Distinguishing Between Fact and Opinion.* San Diego, CA: Greenhaven, 1990.

Source Notes

Adams, Robert. "Smithsonian Horizons." *Smithsonian*, May 1991.

Appelbaum, Richard and Peter Dreier. "American Nightmare: Homelessness." *Challenge,* March/April 1991.

Bingham, Richard D., Roy E. Green, and Sammis B. White. *The Homeless in Contemporary Society.* Newbury Park, CA: Sage Publications, 1987.

Bragg, Rick. "Sleepless in Central Park." *New York Times,* July 24, 1994.

Kirp, David L. "A Sedan Is Not a Home." *Commonweal,* February 12, 1993.

Rubin, Lynda. "Their Hopes, Their Hurts, Their Dreams." *Newsday,* January 27, 1994.

Silverstein, Ken. "Give Me Shelter." *Scholastic Update*, March 11, 1994.

Torrey, E. Fuller. "Who Goes Homeless?" *National Review,* August 26, 1991.

Vargas, Betty. "A Test of Faith." *Essence,* January 1992.

"What Are the Rights of the Homeless? *Glamour,* July 1993.

Index

Photo Credits
Cover and page 46: ©Mark Peterson/SABA; p. 4: ©John Chiasson/Liaison International; p. 7: ©Douglas Burrows/Gamma Liaison; p. 9: ©Jean Marc Giboux/Gamma Liaison; p. 12: ©Stephen Ferry/Gamma Liaison; p. 15: ©Joel Stettenheim/SABA; p. 16: ©Peter Blakely/SABA; p. 19: ©Ralf-Finn Hestoft/SABA; pp. 21, 32, 39, 43, 49: AP/Wide World Photos; p. 24: ©Porter Gifford/Gamma Liaison; p. 29: ©Najlah Feanny/SABA; pp. 34, 37: ©Jon Levy/Gamma Liaison; p. 45: ©Andy Uzzle/Gamma Liaison; p. 48: ©Argo/SABA; p. 53: ©Steve Lehman/SABA; p. 55: ©Shahn Kermani/Gamma Liaison; p. 56: courtesy of Common Meals, Seattle, Washington.

Charts by Blackbirch Graphics, Inc.